WHAT IS THE CHRISTIAN ATTITUDE TO HOMOSEXUALITY?

What Is the Christian Attitude to Homosexuality?

NICKY GUMBEL

KINGSWAY PUBLICATIONS
EASTBOURNE

ISBN 1 84291 057 4

Published by
KINGSWAY COMMUNICATIONS LTD
Lottbridge Drove, Eastbourne, BN23 6NT, England.
Email: books@kingsway.co.uk

Print production for the publishers by
Bookprint Creative Services, P.O. Box 827, BN21 3YJ, England.
Printed in Great Britain.

Contents

What Is the Christian Attitude to Homosexuality?

The Bible is the story of God's love for all humanity. God loves all people, irrespective of race, colour, background or sexual orientation. As we approach this subject, I am conscious of the agony that exists for many people in this area. Jesus came not to condemn us, but to save (John 3:17). In the same way, the Christian community needs to show sensitivity and understanding towards those for whom their homosexual orientation is a daily struggle, and to affirm them as human beings loved by God.

A homosexually orientated person is someone whose sexual preference is for someone of the same sex. Alfred C. Kinsey, in his 1948 survey of white US males, 'Sexual Behaviour in the Human Male', found that 4 per cent were exclusively homosexual, 10 per cent had been homosexual for up to three years and 37 per cent had had some kind of homosexual experience between adolescence and old age.

This produced a popular view that approximately one in ten of the population was homosexual. However, a national survey on sexual behaviour and AIDS in Britain published by HMSO in 1993 found that only 6 per cent of the male respondents had had a sexual experience with another man. Only 3.6 per cent had had anal intercourse with another man and of the last group, two-thirds had also had sexual intercourse with a woman.[1] The incidence of homosexual activity among women is even more rare.

These results conform with a new study of male sexual behaviour – the most thorough carried out in the United States since the Kinsey report. This survey by the Alan Guttmacher Institute showed that only 1 per cent of American men considered themselves exclusively homosexual, although 2 per cent said they had engaged in homosexual activity at one time or another. This contrasts sharply with the popular conception that homosexual activity is quite common. Nevertheless, the issue affects enough people for the question of a Christian attitude to homosexuality to be raised frequently.

We should reject and resist all forms of irrational prejudice. 'This carries with it the duty to be active in protecting those who are victimised, since it is sadly true that members of the gay and lesbian community are all too often not only verbally disparaged and abused or made the targets of cruel so-called "humour", but are also physically assaulted.'[2] AIDS is even seen by some as homosexuals getting their 'just deserts'.

On the other hand, the gay liberation movement outside and within the Christian church 'urge the view that homosexuality is simply a natural variant of human sexuality – as natural as red hair or left-handedness – to be affirmed and rejoiced in, and that its expression in fully loving physical sexual embrace is well within the purpose and will of God.'[3]

What is the Christian attitude to homosexuality? Is homosexual practice an option for the Christian? Is AIDS the judgement of God on homosexual practice? Can homosexual orientation be changed, and is such a change desirable? What should our attitude be to those with a homosexual orientation? These are the questions that are often raised and which I will try to address in this booklet.

IS HOMOSEXUAL PRACTICE AN OPTION FOR A CHRISTIAN?

The biblical view of sexual intercourse is entirely positive and liberating. God created sex for our enjoyment and designed the male and female body to be united in the unique 'one flesh' union of sexual intercourse. God's context for sexual intercourse is lifelong commitment (in marriage) between one man and one woman (Genesis 2:24). This view of marriage and sex, which Jesus quoted and endorsed, rules out all sex outside marriage, whether heterosexual or homosexual. This is so far from the views of many in our society that it is easy to dismiss the biblical view as absurd, unrealistic and obsolete. However, the so-called 'freedom' now acceptable in our sexual behaviour does not necessarily bring with it happiness – and the freedom it promises may in fact be a trap into which many of us risk falling.

9

Homosexual practice is not mentioned often in the Bible but we must face the references that do appear with courage and honesty. As we read Scripture, we need to open our hearts and minds to things we may not want to hear, and perhaps to wrestle with the gap between the experience of our own desires and the reality of biblical teaching. Those of us who do not struggle personally in this area must be sure to read the Bible's teaching on the subject from the context of God's love for all.

The biblical writers clearly disapprove of same-sex sexual practices. Such references as there are are brief but 'uncompromisingly negative'.[4] Homosexual practice is among the list of things that the apostle Paul warns against. His teaching is quite explicit: 'Do you not know that the wicked will not inherit the kingdom of God? Do not be deceived: Neither the sexually immoral nor idolaters nor adulterers nor male prostitutes nor homosexual offenders nor thieves nor the greedy nor drunkards nor slanderers nor swindlers will inherit the kingdom of God' (1 Corinthians 6:9–10). (It is important to note that homosexual practice is only one subject in this list. Others include sexual immorality of any kind, greed and dishonesty.)

The word translated as 'male prostitutes' refers not to prostitutes alone, but generally to the 'passive' partners in homosexual intercourse. The word translated as 'homosexual offenders' refers to the 'active' partners and is the word used again in the list of 'lawbreakers and rebels, the ungodly and sinful, the unholy and irreligious' (1 Timothy 1:9). Paul assumed that homosexual practice would have been abandoned at conversion (1 Corinthians 6:11).

In Paul's view, homosexual practice is one of the results of human rebellion against God. God gives us the freedom to follow our own desires if we so choose.

> Therefore God gave them over in the sinful desires of their hearts to sexual impurity for the degrading of their bodies with one another. They exchanged the truth of God for a lie, and worshipped and served created things rather than the Creator – who is for ever praised. Amen. Because of this, God gave them over to shameful lusts. Even their women exchanged natural relations for unnatural ones. In the same way the men also abandoned natural relations with women and were inflamed with lust for one another. Men committed indecent acts with other men, and received in themselves the due penalty for their perversion (Romans 1:24–27).

Paul is referring back again to the created order and the way in which we are designed. Homosexual practice is not 'natural'; it goes against God's created order. Paul also expressly condemns the attitude of those who 'not only continue to do these very things but also approve of those who practise them' (Romans 1:32).

It is vital to note that nowhere does the Bible condemn homosexual orientation, homosexual feelings or homosexual temptation. Temptation is not sin. Jesus was 'tempted in every way, just as we are – yet was without sin' (Hebrews 4:15). What the Bible condemns is not homosexual preference, but homosexual practice (a distinction we will consider later in this booklet). Jesus took the Scriptures as his authority and if Jesus is our Lord, then we must follow him.

Is AIDS the judgement of God on homosexual practice?

AIDS is one of the biggest health threats to humankind and consequently has brought the issue of homosexuality into sharp focus. The World Health Organisation estimates that 36 million people are infected with the HIV virus worldwide. In Africa more may already be dying from AIDS than from famine. But it is important to note that, worldwide, 70 per cent of all new infections are caused through heterosexual transmission. Even in the UK, where initially heterosexual infection was relatively uncommon, by 1999 the reported number of heterosexual cases of HIV exceeded those of homosexual and drug-user infections. There is still, however, a strong link in popular thinking between homosexuality and AIDS in this country.

Obviously there is nothing in the Bible about AIDS, but we can look at biblical principles and seek to apply them to a modern disease. We have seen that God, in his great love, has given us boundaries in order to protect us. When we cross those boundaries we often get hurt, just as when one puts a finger in the fire it gets burned. God also imposes a penalty for breaking his laws. Earlier theologians made a distinction between these two different types of judgement. First there is the *effectus* of God's judgement: the inevitable result of sin. Secondly, there is the *affectus*: God's personal (though never malicious or, in a bad sense, emotional) reaction against sin.

Let me explain this distinction by using a human analogy.

There is a law against drinking and driving, the purpose of which is to protect road users from getting hurt. I read in a newspaper of a man who drove after he had drunk excessively. He crashed the car and was seriously injured; his best friend, who was a passenger, was killed. A prosecution was brought and he was sent to prison. His injuries and the death of his friend were an *effectus* of breaking the law, while the penalty of the court was an *affectus*.

How are we to see AIDS in the light of this analogy? Is it an *effectus* or an *affectus* of God's judgement? Is it like the injuries the man received, or is it like the punishment of the court?

One day God will judge the world. There will be a penalty to be paid for all sin (the *affectus* of his judgement) – in the same way that the courts punish crimes today. The judgement will be perfectly fair and just. We will either pay the penalty ourselves or, if we have put our trust in Jesus Christ, we will be saved through what he achieved for us on the cross. This is the final judgement which will occur when Jesus returns. In the meantime, God sometimes intervenes to judge now in this life – as in the case of Sodom and Gomorrah (Genesis 19) and Ananias and Sapphira (Acts 5). These supernatural acts of intervening judgement are comparatively rare throughout the Bible.

On the other hand, his judgement in the sense of *effectus* (the inevitable results of sin) is going on all the time. People are getting hurt as a result of God's laws being broken. As in the case of the drunk driver, it is not only the perpetrator of the offence who gets hurt, but there are also 'innocent' casualties like the driver's best friend.

Returning to the question of AIDS, I do not believe that it can be seen as the judgement of God in the sense of an *affectus* – his personal reaction against sin – any more than lung cancer can be seen as his judgement on cigarette smoking. Certainly, it could not be a judgement, in this sense, on homosexuality. As we have seen, 70 per cent of the new infections worldwide are heterosexual, while female homosexuals are in the safest group. It cannot even be seen as a judgement against promiscuity or sex outside marriage, since some are infected through blood transfusions and others inherit it from their parents.

However, it can be seen as the *effectus* of his judgement: the inevitable results of breaking his law. In our analogy, it is the equivalent of the car crash in which both the guilty and the innocent friend were hurt. God's rules were given to protect people from getting hurt. When his laws are broken, it is often not only the law-breaker who is hurt. Sometimes the innocent are hurt also, while others get away with it entirely. Not every drunk driver crashes; not every promiscuous person contracts AIDS or other sexual diseases. Although sooner or later, the drunk driver is likely to have an accident and sooner or later promiscuous sexual activity is likely to lead to hurt. This is due to the way we are made and designed to live, rather than something explosively visited upon us. These activities exceed our physical, emotional and spiritual tolerance and are likely to cause damage in the long run. If we had kept to biblical standards, AIDS would not have spread. The best way to stop it now would be to return to biblical standards.

But AIDS itself is not the real crisis in our society; rather, it is a symptom of the real crisis, which is that men and women have turned their backs on God. We are now seeing the results of this (Romans 1:21).

WHAT IS THE WAY FORWARD?

The New Testament promises total forgiveness through the cross of Christ. Further, for every Christian the power of sin has been broken at the cross. Therefore, there is now no condemnation for the man or woman who repents and seeks to obey Christ (Romans 8:1). Homosexual practice is not the worst sin; nor is it unforgivable. They have been washed clean.

Writing to the Corinthians, Paul says of the 'sexually immoral', 'adulterers', 'male prostitutes' and 'homosexual offenders': 'That is what some of you were. But you were washed, you were sanctified, you were justified in the name of the Lord Jesus Christ and by the Spirit of our God' (1 Corinthians 6:9–11).

By using the past tense, Paul is suggesting that his readers have changed. They have given up their former practices, although some will continue to be tempted in this area throughout their lives. God's promise is that 'no temptation has seized you except what is common among people. And God is faithful; he will not let you be tempted beyond what you can bear. But when you are tempted, he will also provide a way out so that you can stand up under it' (1 Corinthians 10:13).

Tony Campolo writes:

It is *very* important that all of us distinguish between homosexual *orientation* and homosexual *behaviour*. Homosexual orientation is an inclination to desire sexual intimacy with members of the same sex. Homosexual behaviour is 'making love' or seeking sexual gratification through physical interaction with members of the same sex. The first is desire. The second is action. The first is temptation. The second is yielding to temptation.

I personally know many Christians with a homosexual orientation who fight against their desire for homosexual behaviour through the power of the Holy Spirit. The desire to have sexual gratification through physical involvement with persons of their own sex is a constant one with many of them (just as heterosexual desire can be a constant for many), but they are 'more than conquerors through Christ who strengtheneth' them (Romans 8:37).

I cannot help but admire these brave saints who endure lives of sexual frustration because of their commitment to what they believe are biblical admonitions against homosexual intercourse. Many such Christians have told me about their long nights of spiritual agony as they have struggled against the flesh to remain faithful to what they believe to be the will of God. Any who believe that these homosexuals who remain celibate for the sake of Christ are anything less than glorious victors in God's kingdom ought to be ashamed of themselves.[5]

And Christopher Townsend writes:

The life of Christ shows us that neither a committed, exclusive partnership nor sexual experience is essential to personal fulfilment. Jesus, who lived the only perfect human life, was single and celibate. The need not to be 'alone' may be met through friendships without sexual intimacy. Indeed while human sexuality is affirmed by the Bible, its significance is also qualified. Our true humanity does not ultimately rest in our sexuality but in fulfilling our capacity for personal communion with God.[6]

IS IT POSSIBLE FOR OUR SEXUAL ORIENTATION TO BE CHANGED?

This is related to the discussion about what causes homosexual orientation. There are many hypotheses as to the causes, but no absolute conclusions. Some people believe that homosexual orientation is innate or inborn. In spite of some recent claims, there is no conclusive scientific evidence that genetic or hormonal factors are causative in homosexual behaviour. However, there is a great deal of evidence that homosexual orientation is something that may be acquired or learned. It may be caused by a number of factors: lack of love and affirmation from a same-sex parent; a dominant, controlling or overprotective and possessive mother; a weak, ineffective or rejecting father; incest or sexual abuse. All of these are possible causes.

Whatever the causes, in most cases homosexually orientated people are the product of forces over which they have little or no control, certainly in the early stages. Whether the basis is biological or sociological, it is almost certainly not their fault. Of course, we should never condemn anyone for being homosexually orientated. On the other hand, whatever the cause, everyone still has the responsibility to live with their orientation and regulate its expression. Even if there is a scientific basis, it does not mean that it is God's will. Genetic conditioning produces good things such as the wonderful diversity of human beings but also bad things like congenital disease. As we have seen, such things are not part of the original created order, but are an indirect result of sin entering the world. Therefore, as far as possible, we should seek restoration and healing. None of us is perfect now.

It is understandable that the term 'healing' is hard to digest for many. 'How,' they ask, 'can I be healed from the disorder of being myself? Is what I am some kind of disease? Is this not an offensive suggestion and an affront to my identity and self-esteem?' To which we must reply in the words of the St Andrew's Day Statement, 'At the deepest ontological level . . . there can be no such thing as "a" homosexual or "a" heterosexual: there are human beings, male and female, called to a redeemed humanity in Christ.'

Christopher Townsend writes that

> since the fall, sin has been the root cause of a deep state of disorder within human nature. What is found innate in men and women is not necessarily good . . . Further, sin is a power which dominates people and deceives us that we are free. We are all 'slaves to sin' (John 8:34), filled with compelling desires leading us into disobedient actions, living out involuntary but culpable rebellion (see, eg Romans 7:13–25). Those compelling desires are different for different people; for some they are homosexual desires.[7]

In this sense, all of us need healing.

When our Lord Jesus Christ returns, our bodies will be made perfect (Romans 8:23), and all who are in Christ will be totally healed. For some, healing in this area takes place in this life. A British Medical Association survey listed fourteen case histories of homosexually orientated people who were totally released after Christian conversion, and concluded: 'Homosexuals can be so changed through conversion that their sexual desire loses its mastery.'[8]

Some have been changed through the supernatural power of the Spirit or a gradual process of inner healing, which usually involves forgiving and receiving forgiveness for past hurts. For others, healing takes place through the Christian community as they develop relationships within the body of Christ and find affirmation, love and acceptance. Yet others have been helped through psychiatrists or psychologists (some working in this field have sometimes used morally dubious means to alter the orientation, and the end does not justify the means). There is no conflict between prayer and therapy, for there is only one source of all healing. It is up to God to use miraculous or more ordinary means.

The older a person is, the harder it is to change. Like any behavioural pattern, the more it is followed, the more it will become fixed. The psychiatrist John White writes, 'Once I experience physical pleasure with a member of my own sex, I am more likely to want to experience it again. The more frequently I experience it, the more fixed will the pattern become. What I do determines what I am, just as much as what I am determines what I do.'[9]

Although changes in orientation are unusual, there have been some remarkable changes, even where a pattern is apparently fixed. Five years ago, I met a French violinist in his mid-twenties, who was in a relationship with a man ten years older than him. A member of our congregation gave the man a copy of a Christian book and prayed with him that Jesus would reveal himself within twenty-four hours. That evening he and his partner were having supper when he disintegrated in tears, went into his bedroom and there had an extraordinary vision of Jesus. He gave his life to Christ. The next day, I chatted with him in church and asked him what he was going to do about the relationship. He said that he was going to end it. In order to break the news gently he went out and bought a bunch of flowers, the heads of which were closed. He prayed that by the time they were opened, his partner would have become a Christian. His partner had already seen the remarkable changes in his friend and went to see the person with whom he had prayed. They too prayed, and the older man became a Christian. He also had an amazing vision of Jesus – 'the most powerful experience of my life'. He said afterwards, 'For the first time, I really knew love.'

Both these men are still active Christians. The man in his mid-thirties I know well: he is now a fine Christian leader and often prays with others who are in a similar predicament to the one he was in. He tells me that many of the men he prays with have lacked affirmation, often from their father. They have perhaps sought that missing affirmation through sexual relationships with other men. For them, there is great power in receiving forgiveness from God, and then forgiving their father. Forgiveness gives them freedom from the pain of a disappointing or non-existent relationship with their

20

father, as well as the opportunity to receive affirmation from a heavenly Father. They find themselves emptied of bitterness, anger or disappointment and filled with the love of God. The love of God brings with it transformation and freedom.

WHAT SHOULD OUR ATTITUDE BE TO THOSE INVOLVED IN A HOMOSEXUAL LIFESTYLE?

The primary pastoral task of the church in relation to all its members, whatever their self-understanding and mode of life, is to reaffirm the good news of salvation in Christ, forgiveness of sins, transformation of life and incorporation into the holy fellowship of the church. In addressing those who understand themselves as homosexual, the church does not cease to speak as the bearer of this good news. It assists all its members to a life of faithful witness in chastity and holiness, recognising two forms or vocations in which that life can be lived: marriage and singleness (Genesis 2:24; Matthew 19:4–6; 1 Corinthians 7 *passim*).[10]

Although all of us were created in the image of God, we are all fallen human beings. None of us is without sin. Every area of our lives is affected by sin. None of us is in a position to throw stones at others, although the church sadly has a bad history of it. Jesus said to those about to stone a woman guilty of sexual sin, 'Let any one of you who is without sin be the first to throw a stone at her' (John 8:7). The former Archbishop of Canterbury, Robert Runcie, once pointed out in the context of the debate about homosexuality, 'In this earthly tabernacle of Christ's kingdom there are many mansions, and all of them are made of glass.'

Since he was without sin, Jesus was the one person there in a position to throw stones, but he did not. Rather, he showed her great love and compassion. But he also said to her, 'Go now and leave your life of sin' (John 8:11). Our calling is to follow Christ's example, which is to love and accept people unconditionally. At the same time, we must recognise sin as sin, rather than condone it.

This is a unique combination. Generally the attitude towards homosexuality tends to fall into one of two opposite extremes. On the one hand, there are those who, in accepting the people, *condone* the sin. They say there is nothing wrong with homosexual practice. On the other hand, there are those who condemn the people involved and are personally hostile. 'The story of the Church's attitude to homosexually-orientated people has too often been one of prejudice, ignorance and oppression. All of us need to acknowledge that, and to repent for any part we may have had in it.'[11]

We are called to love those living a homosexual lifestyle. But love does not involve condoning sin. Indeed, the opposite is the case. If we see a child about to run across a road and shout, 'Don't!', it is not because we want to ruin their fun. We warn them because we love them and we don't want them to get hurt. In the same way, we are called to speak out, when appropriate, against the practice of homosexuality. It is wrong to promote a homosexual lifestyle in schools. It is wrong to ordain unrepentant, practising homosexuals into Christian leadership.

On the other hand, we are called to love people and

22

welcome them with open arms into the church. As John Stott writes, 'At the heart of the homosexual condition is a deep loneliness, the natural human hunger for mutual love, a search for identity, and a longing for completeness. If homosexual people cannot find these things in the local "church family", we have no business to go on using that expression.'[12]

We must never lose sight of the fact that homosexually orientated people 'are in every way as valuable to and as valued by God as heterosexually orientated people. God loves us all alike, and has for each one of us a range of possibilities within his design for the universe . . . Every human being has a unique potential for Christlikeness, and an individual contribution to make through that likeness to the final consummation of all things.'[13]

We need to promote a safe environment where the homosexually orientated can find somebody with whom they can talk and pray. Many have never been able to tell anyone about their internal battles. The ability to talk to someone about their struggle is often the first step to bringing light into the darkness.

Further, the church should be at the forefront of bringing hope and healing to those with AIDS and HIV. A fine example is ACET (AIDS Care Education and Training), which seeks to minister to those in our society with AIDS by providing practical help in a non-judgemental way. The organisation encourages those with HIV/AIDS to think positively about their future and also educates young people in order to prevent them from becoming infected.

Love is the key from first to last. It was God who, in his

love, gave us sex. In his love, he also gave us boundaries. His heart must break when he sees the mess we have got ourselves into. In his love he sent Jesus to bring us forgiveness and the power to resist temptation and also to bring change. We are called to be like him and to go out and love as he loved us.

FOR FURTHER READING

John Stott, *Issues Facing Christians Today* (Marshall Pickering, 1984), chapter 16.
Martin Hallett, *I Am Learning to Love* (Marshall Pickering, 1987).

NOTES

1. E. G. Knox, C. MacArthur and K. J. Simons, 'Sexual Behaviour and AIDS in Britain' (HMSO, 1993), p84.
2. 'Issues in Human Sexuality – A Statement by the House of Bishops of the General Synod of the Church of England', December 1991, p34, para 4.8.
3. David Atkinson, *Pastoral Ethics in Practice* (Monarch, 1989), p74.
4. Oliver O'Donovan, *The Way Forward?* Edited by Timothy Bradshaw, p28.
5. Tony Campolo, *20 Hot Potatoes Christians Are Afraid to Touch* (Word Publishing, 1988), p110.
6. Christopher Townsend, 'Homosexuality: Finding the Way of Truth and Love' *Cambridge Papers* Vol 3 No.2 1994, p3.
7. *Ibid.*
8. *Homosexuality and Prostitution* (BMA, 1955), p92.

9. John White, *Eros Defiled* (IVP, 1978), p111.
10. The St Andrew's Day Statement, *An Examination of the Theological Principles Affecting the Homosexuality Debate*, 30 November 1995. Numerous writers – published by CCLEC.
11. 'Issues in Human Sexuality – A Statement by the House of Bishops of the General Synod of the Church of England', December 1991, p48, para 5.24.
12. John Stott, *New Issues Facing Christians Today* (Marshall Pickering, 1999), p417.
13. 'Issues in Human Sexuality – A Statement by the House of Bishops of the General Synod of the Church of England', December 1991, p41, para 5.4.

Alpha

This book is an Alpha resource. The Alpha course is a practical introduction to the Christian faith initiated by Holy Trinity Brompton in London, and now being run by thousands of churches throughout the UK as well as overseas.

For more information on Alpha, and details of tapes, videos and training manuals, contact the Alpha office, Holy Trinity Brompton on 0207 581 8255, (home page: http://www.alpha.org.uk), or STL, PO Box 300, Kingstown Broadway, Carlisle, Cumbria CA3 0QS.

Alpha Hotline for telephone orders:
0845 7581 278 (all calls at local rate)

To order from overseas:
Tel +44 1228 512512
Fax +44 1228 514949

Kingsway Publications

Alpha

Alpha titles available

Why Jesus?   A booklet given to all participants at the start of the Alpha course. 'The clearest, best illustrated and most challenging short presentation of Jesus that I know.' – Michael Green

Why Christmas?   The Christmas version of *Why Jesus?*

Questions of Life   The Alpha course in book form. In fifteen compelling chapters Nicky Gumbel points the way to an authentic Christianity which is exciting and relevant to today's world.

A Life Worth Living   What happens after Alpha? Based on the book of Philippians, this is an invaluable next step for those who have just completed the Alpha course, and for anyone eager to put their faith on a firm biblical footing.

Telling Others: The Alpha Initiative   The theological principles and the practical details of how courses are run. Each alternate chapter consists of a testimony of someone whose life has been changed by God through an Alpha course.

Challenging Lifestyle   Studies in the Sermon on the Mount showing how Jesus' teaching flies in the face of modern lifestyle and presents us with a radical alternative.

30 Days   Nicky Gumbel selects thirty passages from the Old and New Testament which can be read over thirty days. It is designed for those on an Alpha course and others who are interested in beginning to explore the Bible.

The Heart of Revival   Ten Bible studies based on the book of Isaiah, drawing out important truths for today by interpreting some of the teaching of the Old Testament prophet Isaiah. The book seeks to understand what revival might mean and how we can prepare to be part of it.

All titles are by Nicky Gumbel, who is on the staff of
Holy Trinity Brompton